MW00916521

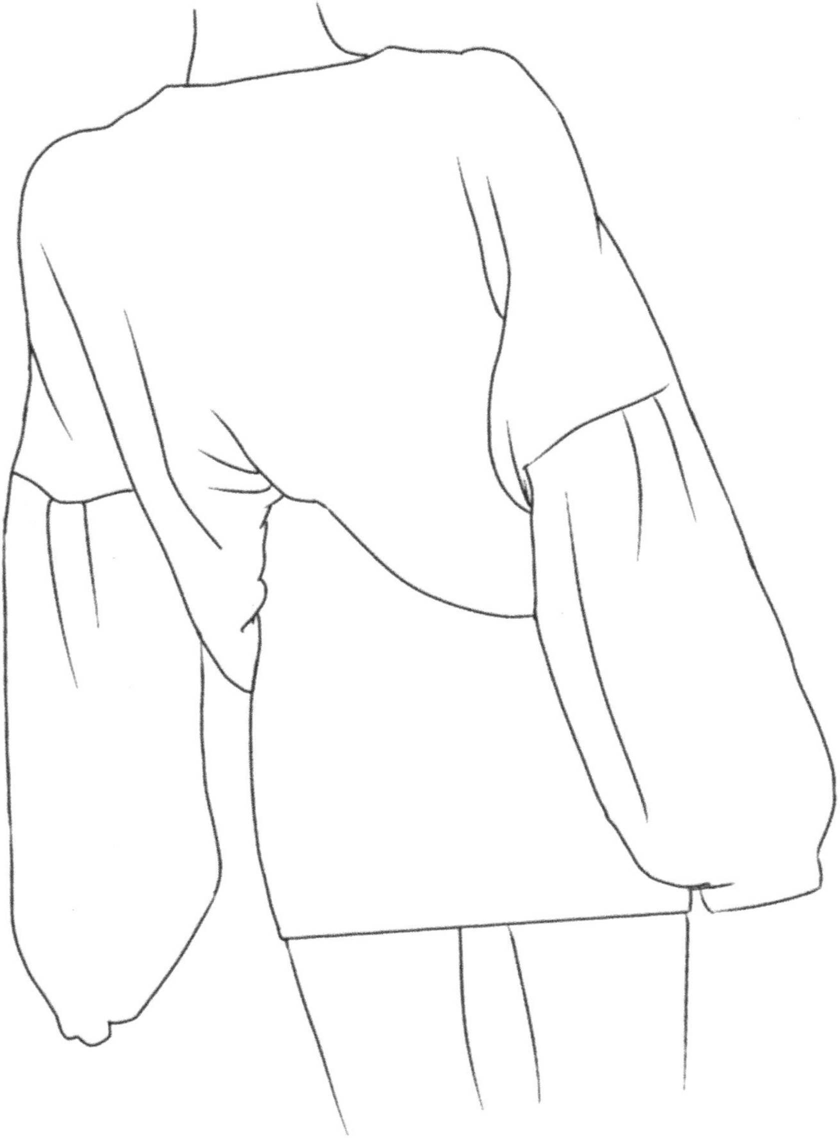

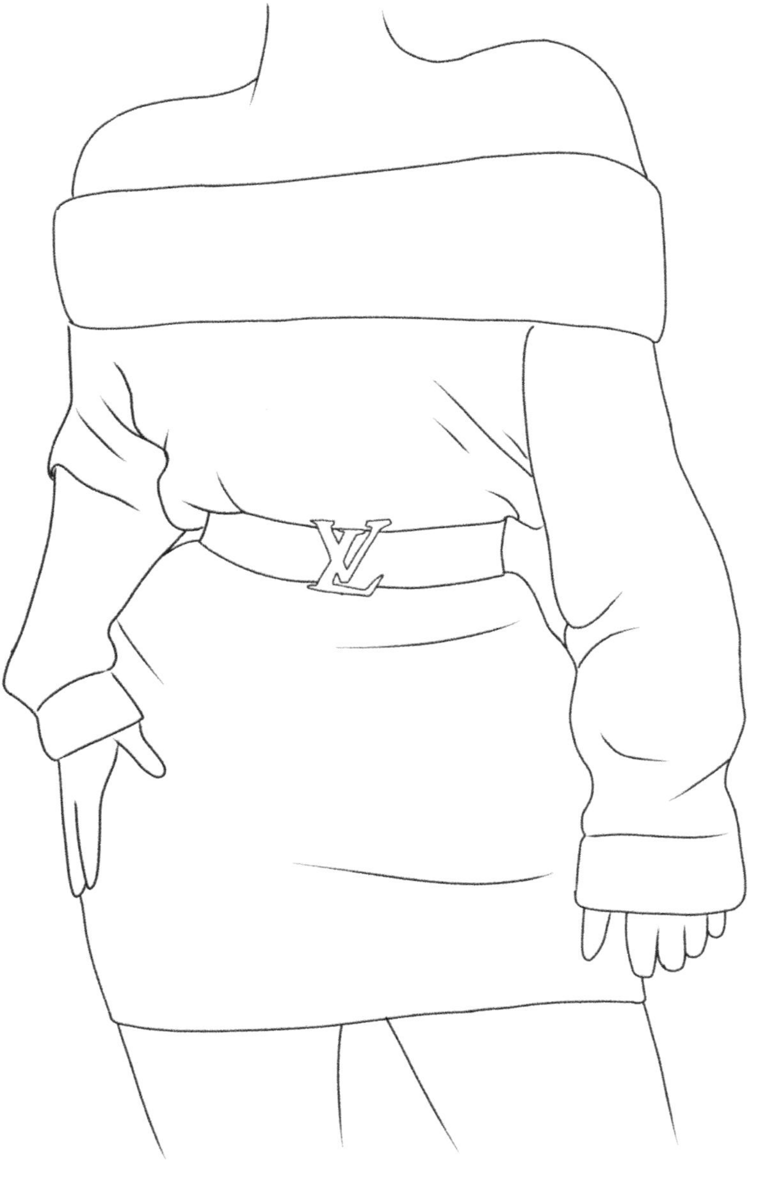

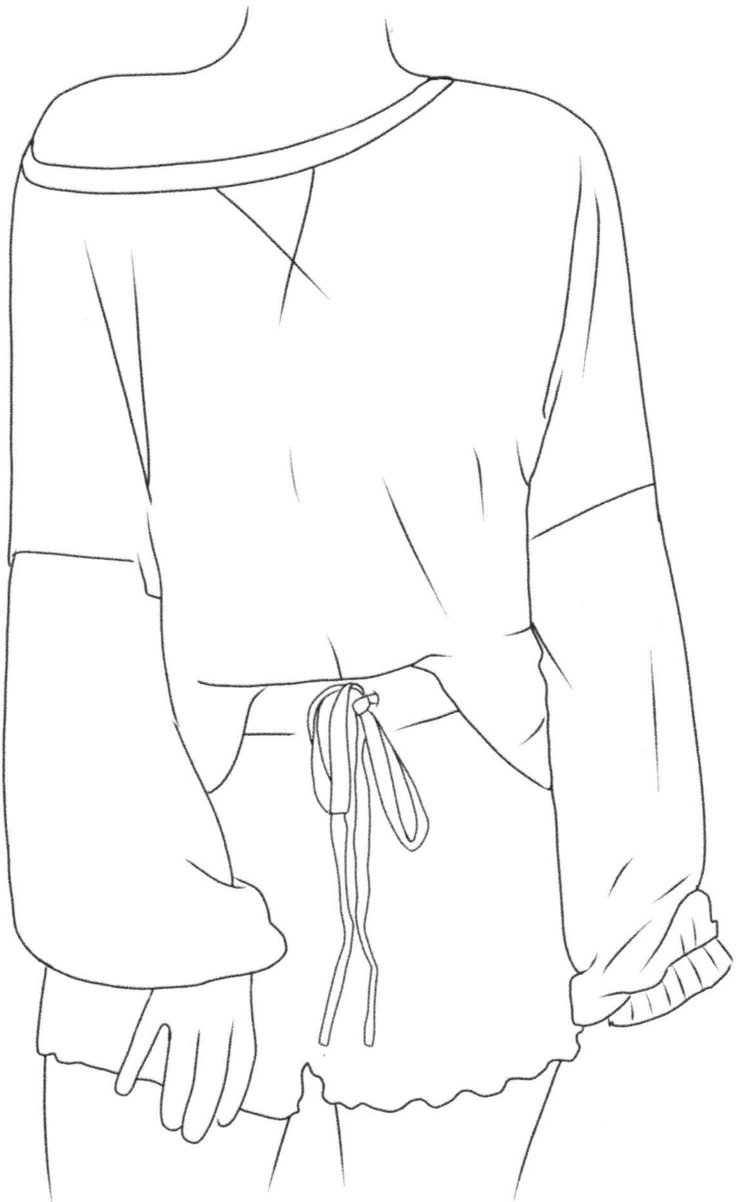

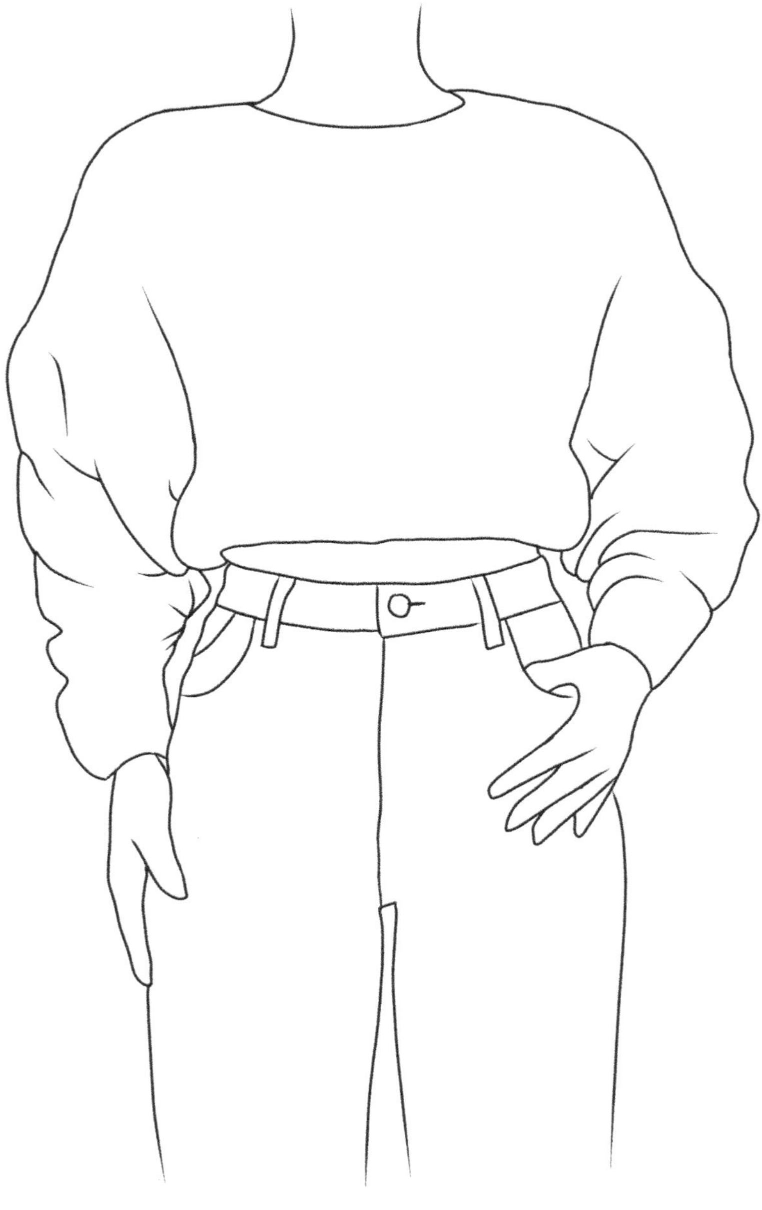

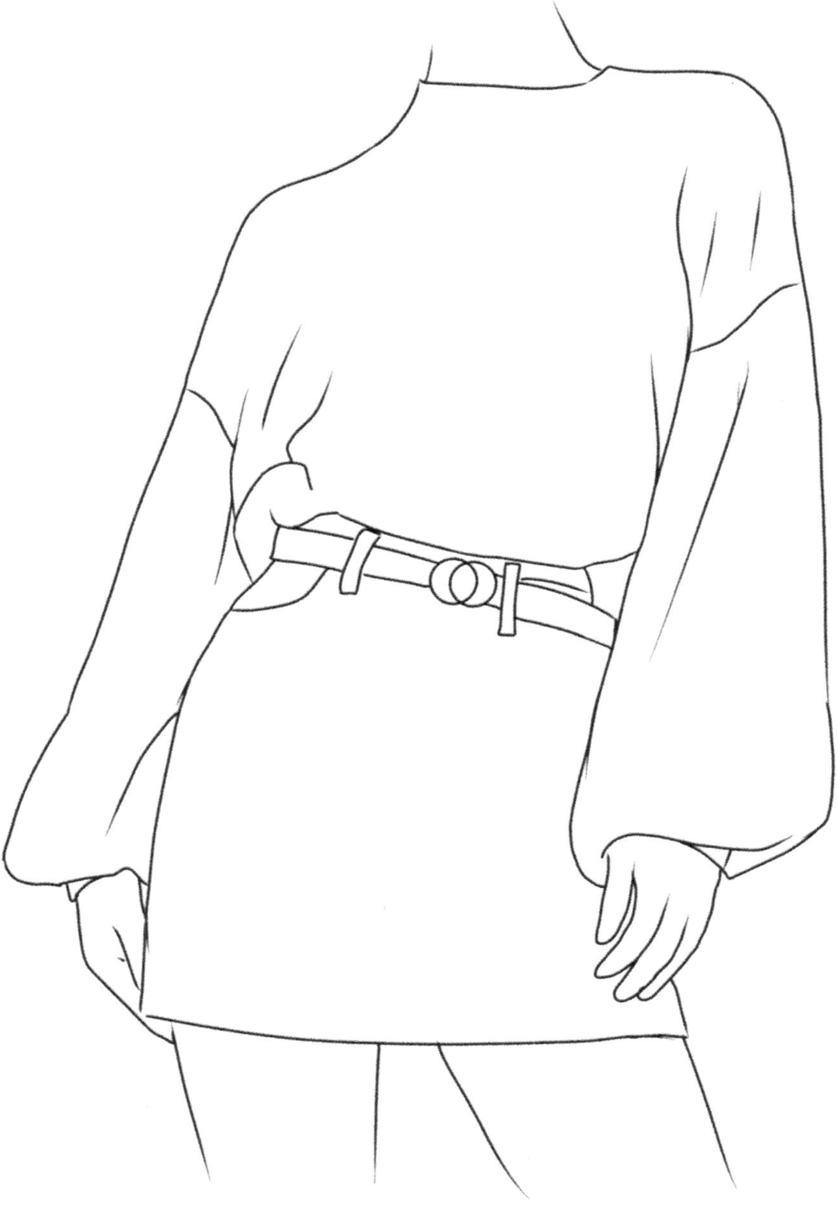

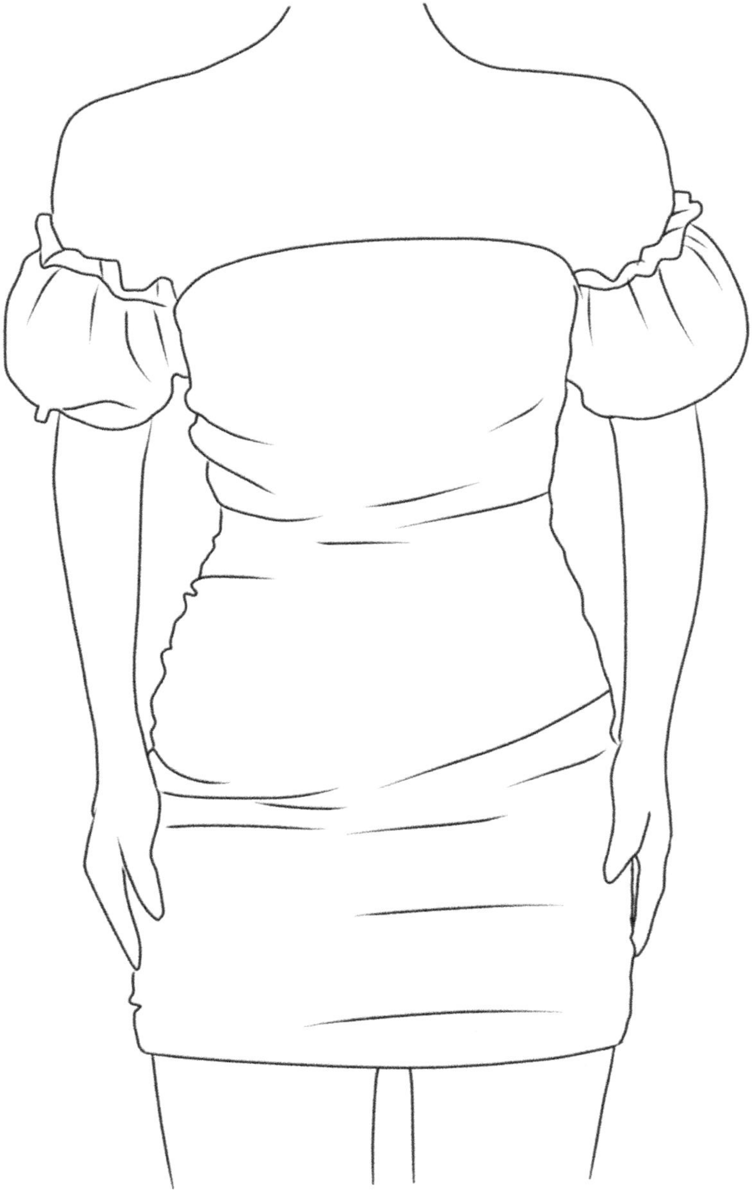

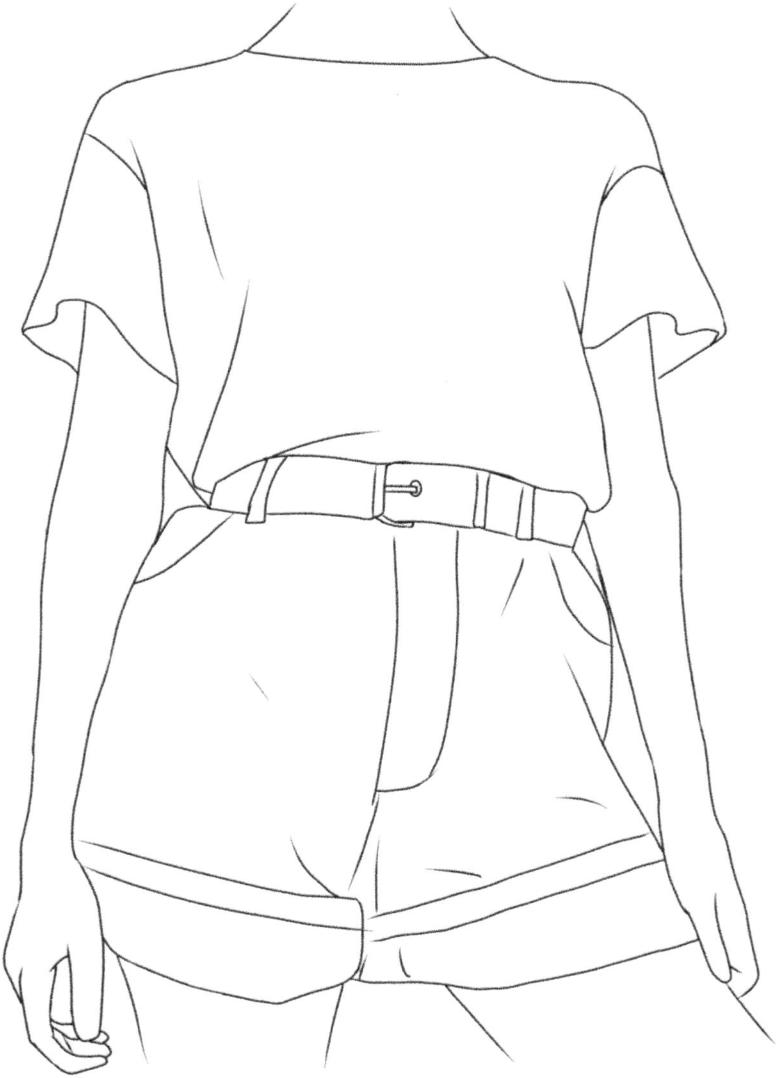

ISBN: 9798562767196

Socials
Instagram: @nooralmahdi_art
TikTok: @nooralmahdi_art
YouTube: Noor Almahdi

Made in the USA
Las Vegas, NV
24 November 2021

35095771R00046